Growing... Plants, Functional Skills, and Communication Skills in School Gardens

A Public School Guide to Gardening Activities for Students with Autism and Other Special Needs

Tammy Blake, OTD, OTR/L
Dawn Leach, MS, CCC-SLP
Shannon Fenix, MS, OTR/L

© 2014 Tammy Blake, Dawn Leach, and Shannon Fenix
All Rights Reserved.

No part of this publication may be reproduced, stored in a retrieval system, or transmitted, in any form or by any means, electronic, mechanical, photocopying, recording, or otherwise, without the written permission of the author.

First published by Dog Ear Publishing
4010 W. 86th Street, Ste H
Indianapolis, IN 46268
www.dogearpublishing.net

ISBN: 978-1-4575-2633-6

This book is printed on acid-free paper.

Printed in the United States of America

To our students with special needs for affording us the opportunity to grow with them and create this resource guide as an invitation for students and teachers to expand their learning environments and establish an appreciation of nature

Contents

Acknowledgments 5

Preface 6

Developing Public School Gardens 7

Safety Precautions 9

Accommodations 11

Guiding Models and Student Objectives 12

Garden Jobs 17

Autumn Activities 33

Winter Activities 45

Spring Activities 53

Summer Activities 65

Garden Leisure Activities 73

Appendix 81

Bibliography 109

Acknowledgments

The authors wish to express their gratitude to those who journeyed with us to enhance learning for all students and who engaged in the mission of creating an environment that fosters independence, stewardship of the environment, and high academic standards.

To Elaine Tholen for sharing her knowledge of gardening and outdoor learning environments, embracing students with special needs, having the foresight to see gardening as a powerful learning tool for all students, and quietly inspiring others to venture outdoors.

To the school administration and the parent-teacher association for initiating the development of gardens, habitats, and sanctuaries.

To the parent-teacher association for funding the outdoor learning environment.

To Nancy Suleiman, Melissa Modarressi, and Laurie Andrews for embracing outdoor learning and their commitment to providing therapeutic interventions and learning experiences to their students with autism.

To the school staff for taking on the endeavor of involving all grade levels and constructing additional gardens for the school as a showcase of learning to the community and visitors.

To the students, parents, and community volunteers for caring for the gardens throughout the year by watering and weeding the plants, providing birdseed, building the raised beds, mulching, and providing other supports.

To Meghan Leach for creating the cover and listening to endless suggestions for edits and ideas.

To Helen Leach for editing support.

To Jo Anne Culross for providing data entry and moral support.

To our family and friends for being supportive and encouraging us.

To our exceptional students who learned that it is OK to get dirty, play in the dirt, play with worms, get wet, take turns, and care for the environment. We thank you for being our canvas for new ideas that inspired this book.

Preface

As a therapeutic intervention, gardening has been used in a variety of settings with people of all ages (American Horticultural Therapy Association, 2013). The integration of people and activity into the natural environment anchors language, communication, function, and mobility to real-life experiences. These real-life experiences are crucial factors for learning and for the generalization of life skills for students with special needs.

Students with special needs often become observers and bystanders in their own environments; therefore, it is essential to facilitate their participation, functional skills, and communication as active learners. Gardening as a medium to teach academic skills, model social skills, and practice fine motor and gross motor skills, as well as embark on a pursuit of possible lifetime leisure or skilled employment, is an invaluable tool.

Developing outdoor learning environments and gardens, especially within a public school setting, is an ongoing and evolving process. The focal points for the initial proposal to administrators should include state standards of learning, core curriculum, and individualized education plans that incorporate academic instruction, communication and language development, social learning and interactions, stewardship, and school-community relationships.

This collection of authentic activities incorporates gardening and garden-related tasks as a mode to foster student growth, learning, and independence in a safe environment.

Developing Public School Gardens

Why are school gardens becoming a popular method of teaching? Gardens and outdoor learning environments provide unparalleled opportunities to bridge standards of learning and real-life experiences, as well as invite students to explore a variety of healthy food choices and leisure activities. Gardening offers hands-on learning activities, which are engaging for students, and provides an opportunity to frontload vocabulary, in addition to supporting text to real-world connections, thereby helping students generate questions.

How do school gardens benefit learning?

- Learning styles: Garden activities incorporate multimodality learning and provide a safe milieu for students to explore their environment and expand their comfort zone to promote learning (Dekker, Lee, Howard-Jones, and Jolles, 2012).

- Curriculum connections: The academic curricula in math, science, history, social studies, art, language arts, and technology all yield opportunities for interactive learning and investigation of concepts via life activities.

- Career development and exploration: Students with special education needs can acquire pre-work and work-related skills by learning how to use tools safely and effectively; learning work behaviors, such as staying in a location, initiating and completing a task, following directions, and restoring work areas; and exploring new tasks and skill concepts.

- Psychological benefits: Throughout history, the benefits of outdoor environments and gardening have been immeasurable and have been illustrated and well documented in research (American Horticultural Therapy Association, 2013). Currently, gardening is reemerging in hospitals, nursing homes, prisons, adolescent centers, and veterans' hospitals and rehabilitation centers as a therapeutic intervention for posttraumatic stress disorder, depression, anxiety, stress reduction, and other psychological diagnoses (Husted, 2012).

  - Students and staff: Rigorous educational demands and high expectations are placed on students and staff daily. The engagement of students and staff in the outdoor learning spaces "helps improve memory, cognitive abilities, task initiation, language skills, socialization and people learn to work independently, problem solve, and follow directions" (American Horticultural Therapy Association, 2013). Nature also "provides an opportunity for healing and stress reduction and their sense of well-being increases" (Chicago Botanic Garden, 2013, *Horticultural Therapy Services*). Research has also shown that gardening and outdoor learning environments "elicit positive psychological and emotional responses by relieving stress, providing a nonthreatening atmosphere, alleviating depression, and helping people connect with nature" (Chicago Botanic Garden, 2013, *Horticultural Therapy Services*).

- Community: School grounds that are well maintained add to the aesthetics of the community, making it a more desirable place in which to live. Garden spaces spur community involvement, "[reduce] crime, [reduce] city heat from streets and parking lots, and [stimulate] social interactions" (American Community Gardening Association, 2013) in addition to encouraging students to care for their school community and their neighborhood community (American Community Gardening Association, 2013). Students who care for both their school and neighborhood communities take pride in the appearance of both and encourage others to show respect and civic responsibility.

- Learning communities: The outdoor learning environment encourages student participation in the larger school community, thus facilitating a kinship and investment in the community. This association fosters "increased physical, emotional and social well-being and enhanced quality of life" (Hoogsteen and Woodgate, 2010, p. 325). This symbiotic relationship of social participation, emotional health, and learning communities nurtures individual growth (Hoogsteen and Woodgate, 2010; Laverdure and Rose, 2012).

Many school groups start small gardens and outdoor learning environments. The process takes time to plan and initiate and is ongoing, building from year to year. Developing an outdoor learning environment requires administrative support, motivated staff, and funding.

When getting started, the school group should have a conversation with the administrator about the benefits of gardening and about how learning and curriculum connect to the outdoor environment. Representatives from the school group and the administrator should examine the school grounds to identify a small starting space, such as flower beds, flowerpots, and decorative vegetation that currently exist around the school.

The garden can be expanded each year with the addition of new spaces. Some helpful ideas include butterfly gardens for the life cycle of the butterfly and for science experiments; wildlife habitats such as bird sanctuaries for environmental awareness, learning about living and nonliving things, producers and consumers, warm-blooded and cold-blooded creatures, and observational learning; and woodland theaters for outdoor reading and interactive plays. Additional garden ideas include flower gardens for the study of plants, including plant parts and their functions; herb gardens for sensory exploration and food experiments; vegetable gardens for diet and nutrition education and healthy food tastings; sensory gardens for self-awareness and personal preferences; and themed gardens with connections to the curriculum such as a regional history lesson or literature lesson.

The outdoor learning environment and gardens can be supported by volunteers such as local children and teen clubs, the local school community, and organizations that utilize the school. Volunteer schedules are easily managed with electronic communications and calendars.

Funding

There are many avenues for funding, such as donations, grants, allocated school funds, parent-teacher association support, and corporate partnerships. Funding is an essential part of developing and maintaining a healthy garden and outdoor learning environment.

Now, *get growing!* Start your own outdoor learning environment and garden!

Safety Precautions

Safety precautions are an important part of the outdoor learning environment. Students can be allergic to a variety of known and unknown items such as environmental allergens, insect bites, and food items, especially if they have not been exposed to a variety of foods.

Students may also be sensitive to heat and cold, direct sunlight to the skin, or indirect sunlight to the eyes and may need to wear protective clothing such as gloves, long-sleeved shirts, and sunglasses. They may also have a need for hydration during the outdoor activities, and water should be available.

The safe use of tools and supplies is a requirement for participating in the outdoor learning environment and gardening. Tools come in a variety of lengths, weights, and sizes; they may have sharp edges and pointed tips and can cause injury if not properly handled.

Safety precautions and procedures are not only an important part of the outdoor learning environment and gardening tasks but also an important life skill. Safety awareness needs to be taught early and reviewed frequently so that it becomes a habit for leisure activities and work environments.

Individual Allergies

All adults directly supervising students should be aware of students' known allergies. Some students may have on file official emergency care plans that include the use of inhalers and epinephrine auto-injector pens.

Some common symptoms of allergies to be aware of are sudden difficulty breathing or wheezing, swelling of the lips or tongue, difficulty swallowing, itching, a tingling sensation, a metallic taste in the mouth, feelings of apprehension or agitation, and vomiting. Vomiting may occur with or without any of the above symptoms (Centers for Disease Control and Prevention, 2013, *Glossary*).*

* The school health coordinator needs to be aware of any noted symptoms. Emergency professionals may need to be contacted. This is informational in nature and not meant to be a comprehensive list of symptoms. By consulting the school health coordinator, additional information can be gathered.

Proper Care of Tools and Supplies

Properly maintained tools are essential. Tools should be cleaned of dirt and debris prior to temporary or seasonal storage. To maintain integrity, metal tools should be cleaned and oiled thoroughly. Seeds and soil should be stored in waterproof, sealed containers to help maintain their vitality (Better Homes and Gardens, 2012, *How to Care for Garden Tools*).

Tool Safety

Having a list of rules and expected behavior during outdoor learning activities promotes a clear understanding of the guidelines for the students. Students should know the rules and adhere to them at all times. Prior to activities, especially when tools are utilized, rules should be reviewed.

Tool safety practices:

1. Walk while carrying tools and supplies.
2. Designate an area near the garden activity where tools can be safely stored while not in use.
3. Choose the best tool for the job by determining the type and size of tool.
4. Carry tools by the handle with sharp tips and edges toward the ground.
5. During short periods of time when tools are not in use, turn tool tips and edges toward the ground.
6. Prevent trips and falls by taking care to return tools to the designated area (Better Homes and Gardens, 2012, *How to Care for Garden Tools*).

Environmental Considerations

Temperature is subjective and can affect a student's level of participation. In cooler weather, students may need to wear jackets or gloves to engage effectively in the garden activities. Alternatively, if it is too warm, students may need to work in the shade or wear hats for protection.

Hydration is important for the health and well-being of adults and students; dehydration occurs faster in warm and humid climates. Throughout an activity, water breaks should be encouraged.

Sunscreen or protective clothing should be worn year round when working outside (American Academy of Dermatology, 2013, *Sunscreen FAQs*).

Accommodations

Universal Design
Universal design concepts should be implemented in the planning of the outdoor learning environment and garden. This will afford all students, teachers, and community members the opportunity to access and utilize these environments.

Definition of Universal Design
> Universal design is the design of products and environments to be usable by all people, to the greatest extent possible, without the need for adaptation or specialized design.
>
> The intent of universal design is to simplify life for everyone by making products, communications and the built environment more usable by as many people as possible at little or no extra cost. Universal design benefits people of all ages and abilities. (Office of Special Education and Rehabilitative Services, 2008, *Frequently Asked Questions about NIDRR*)

Some considerations for universal design include pathways and walkways; height and width of garden beds and raised beds, including vertical beds; and types of tools and tool handles. The pathways should be wide, sloped, level, well-drained, and firm.

> Paths need to be 36 inches wide for a wheelchair, 5 feet wide for two people to walk side by side. A five foot turn around area is required for wheelchairs. The water spigots should be appropriate height and easily accessible. A lever handle [on spigots] is advantageous because it can be operated without a tight grasp or twisting. Tools that are lightweight, made from plastic or light metal such as aluminum are less tiring to use. Long-handled tools offer greater leverage and are critical for gardening from a seated position. Telescopic tools that can be adjusted to various lengths are designed to allow gardeners to reach into the garden bed from a seated position. Additionally, tools that are ergonomically designed assist with grasp and control. (Community Action Coalition for South Central Wisconsin, Inc., 2013, *Madison's Inclusive Community Gardens*)

Visual Strategies
"Use tools with brightly colored handles or paint or tape the handles in a contrasting color to provide contrast for gardeners with low vision" (Community Action Coalition for South Central Wisconsin, Inc., 2013, *Madison's Inclusive Community Gardens*). The use of large-print materials, pictures, symbols, braille, and an auditory interpretation system can support all ages and learners and learning styles (Community Action Coalition for South Central Wisconsin, Inc., 2013).

Managing Student Behavior
As noted in the chapter on safety, it is helpful to make a list of rules and expected behavior during outdoor learning activities so students will have a clear understanding of the guidelines. The activities and experiences in outdoor learning environments can be a powerful reinforcement for some students and anxiety-producing events for others. Students with behavior-management plans or who are responsive to token systems in the classroom should utilize these systems when learning is extended into the outdoor learning community.

Guiding Models and Student Objectives

The Individuals with Disabilities Education Improvement Act (IDEA) is a federal law which provides the foundation from which public school systems educate students with disabilities (U.S. Department of Education, 2006). Public school agencies are charged with providing an appropriate education for students with disabilities which includes active participation in learning, social engagement with peers, and involvement in the school community.

Outdoor learning and gardening is a means for students with special needs to access learning in a meaningful and purposeful way, facilitating engagement with peers and the school community. To facilitate accessibility to outdoor learning and gardening for students with special needs, highly structured interventions based on solid theory are necessary.

For best practice to be exercised in the public school setting, educational models and occupational therapy models should be employed as the guidelines for outdoor learning and gardening activities.

The educational effect of pre-teaching strategies, skills practice, and post-activity analysis are vital and directly proportional to the acquisition of new knowledge. The outdoor learning environment and gardens provide a bridge for students to apply factual knowledge to conceptual knowledge with hands-on experiences, thereby fortifying understanding (Bransford, Brown, and Cocking, 2002).

An Educational Model

Research indicates that structured learning yields specific connections between past and current learning while laying a foundation for future learning. With implementation of the LEARN Model, an educational model for structuring lesson plans and activities, into outdoor learning and gardening, students benefit by the synthesis of past and present learning. Students analyze their thoughts and actions throughout the tasks and recognize their strengths and challenges while scaffolding skills that may be altered naturally throughout the task, thus increasing competency and building independence (Bransford, Brown, and Cocking, 2002).

A Model for Developing Vocabulary

The terms and definitions used within outdoor learning and gardening activities and teaching may be unfamiliar to students. Utilizing the Frayer Model, a graphic organizer to help build vocabulary, outdoor learning and gardening terminology can be paired and linked to words that are familiar to the student, as well as assist in classifying and comprehending unfamiliar vocabulary. The use of the Frayer Model graphic organizer also serves as a visual reference to facilitate storage and retrieval of vocabulary (WETA, 2013). Incorporating these novel terms into the students' repertoire of functional vocabulary is paramount and is directly related to their ability to incorporate functional learning into the academic setting, thereby increasing the probability of academic achievement (Carleton and Marzano, 2010).

Occupational Therapy Models
Meaningful participation in educational activities, socialization, leisure tasks, and functional tasks is a crucial element for developing life skills and roles in students with autism and other special needs. School-based occupational therapy, speech therapy, and physical therapy services are provided as a means to "ensure that a student can access and participate effectively in school activities of choice and benefit from learning opportunities" (Laverdure and Rose, 2012, p. 349).

Model for Educationally Relevant Services
In the Model for Educationally Relevant Services, therapists merge their knowledge of "health conditions and body functions and structures with the educational process" (Laverdure and Rose, 2012, p. 348). This allows for an alternate approach to previously inaccessible areas of participation in the educational realm. Thus, therapists are

> facilitating activity engagement to build collaborative partnerships with students, families, and teachers and foster family connections with the school context which fosters participation, learning, autonomy, empowerment, belonging, self-efficacy, and skills for community engagement. (Laverdure and Rose, 2012, p. 348).

Person-Environment-Occupation-Performance Model
The Person-Environment-Occupation-Performance (PEOP) Model is a

> client centered model organized to improve the everyday performance of necessary and valued occupations of individuals, organizations, and populations and their meaningful participation in the world around them. This model describes an interaction of person factors (intrinsic factors, including psychological/emotional factors, cognition, neurobehavioral, and physiological factors, as well as spirituality) and environmental factors (extrinsic factors, including social support, societal policies and attitudes, natural and built environments, and cultural norms and values) that either support, enable, or restrict the performance of the activities, tasks, and roles of the individual, organization, or community. (Christiansen, Baum, and Bass-Haugen, 2005, p. 244).

The PEOP Model identifies the fundamental building blocks that are essential in eliciting occupational performance and participation (Christiansen, Baum, and Bass-Haugen, 2005). As each element is unique to each individual, organization, or community, so are the outcomes, the intensity and quality of participation and occupational performance.

Summary of Educational and Occupational Therapy Models
In outdoor learning and gardening, the Frayer Model, the Model for Educationally Relevant Services, and the Person-Environment-Occupation-Performance Model form a synergy that is evident by the students' participation, functional performance outcomes, increased socialization and communication, increased knowledge and skills, and increased self-esteem and confidence. The students actively engage in learning, demonstrating the operational amalgamation of the educational models and the occupational therapy models.

Student Objectives

Each student's needs and learning objectives vary greatly. The following objectives are examples of the possibilities for learning targets that can be used during the learning process while students engage in gardening and garden-related activities.

- Engage students in the larger school community.

- The sensory experience of being outdoors.

- Transition between school spaces.

- Transport materials.

- Develop a variety of grasps, coordination, bilateral skills, fine-motor and gross-motor skills, visual perceptual skills, visual-motor coordination, basic activities of daily living skills (ADLS), and motor-planning skills.

- Develop learning for students to learn skills to include attending to a task, imitating others, following simple and complex directions, functioning in a small group, and learning to wait.

- Develop early learning skills such as labeling, sorting, and matching.

- Promote self-regulation skills through multisensory experiences that include heavy work and a variety of textures.

- Facilitate and promote communication, social interaction, and collaboration from student to student, student to staff, staff to staff, and school to community.

- Encourage students to notice, focus on, and explore their environment, using their sensory systems (tactile, vision, auditory, olfactory, and taste).

- Develop social skills and the ability to share materials through participation in turn-taking with peers.

- Encourage functional communication.

- Develop oral language skills, including vocabulary skills, in students by teaching them to comprehend and express the names of tools, tasks, plants, animals, objects, and the use of peer and adult names and titles.

- Teach students to use oral and written communication skills and vocabulary (ask and answer "wh" questions, identify colors, identify shapes, count, measure, label, match, sort, define, describe, compare and contrast).

- Make connections to text, self, and world.

- Encourage self-advocacy (i.e. asking for materials, tools, assistance, and the like).

- Encourage self-expression through a variety of methods.

- Promote choice making.
- Encourage problem solving.
- Encourage the use of school tools (pencil, pen, crayons, scissors, glue, etc.).
- Develop fine-motor manipulation, finger isolation, and functional grasps.
- Incorporate bilateral coordination.
- Promote task initiation, participation, and completion, including transitioning to and/or predicting the next task.
- Encourage cleanup and restoration of an area after a task.
- Encourage observation and attention to details through drawing and writing journals.
- Encourage drawing, handwriting, spelling, editing, typing, and journaling.
- Encourage approximation in measurement.
- Develop functional use of outdoor tools (trowel, rake, hose, water can, etc.).
- Encourage good stewardship of the environment by respecting living and nonliving things, recycling and up-cycling.
- Have fun!

Garden Jobs

TOOL SAFETY

MATERIALS

- A variety of garden tools (e.g., broom, bucket, water can, trowel, gloves, shovel, rake)
- "Tool Stop" sign: a sign that designates an area where tools can be placed while not in use during an activity (the tool-gathering area)
- Pictures of tools
- Pictures of safe handling of tools

DIRECTIONS

1. Pre-teach targeted vocabulary (names of tools).
2. Transition to the garden shed, where tools are stored.
3. Identify, review, and label all tools and their uses (e.g., a broom is used for sweeping; a shovel is used for digging).
4. Demonstrate safe handling of tools.
5. Involve students in rehearsing safe handling of tools in close proximity to the shed.
6. Direct students to transport tools and the "Tool Stop" sign to the gardening area safely.
7. Have students place the "Tool Stop" sign to mark the area where tools are placed while not in use during the gardening process.
8. Direct students to restore the work area and safely transport tools to the garden shed.

Students must consistently demonstrate safe handling of tools in order to transport and utilize tools independently.

GARDEN JOBS

MATERIALS
- A variety of garden tools (e.g., broom, bucket, water can, trowel, gloves, hose)
- Pictures of tools and garden objects (e.g., bird bath, bird feeder, planter)
- Vocabulary words

DIRECTIONS
1. Pre-teach targeted vocabulary.
2. Have students match and/or identify the various garden tools and garden objects.
3. Observe garden jobs and uses of garden objects.
    a. Water plants
    b. Fill bird bath
    c. Spread mulch
    d. Sweep mulch from walkways or blacktop areas
    e. Plant
    f. Harvest
    g. Trim
    h. Weed
    i. Remove trash
    j. Fill bird feeders
4. Direct students to perform an identified task (as listed above) in correct sequence as detailed by the teacher or via student checklist.
5. Direct students to restore the work area.

CLEAN AND FILL THE BIRD BATH

MATERIALS
- Sponges
- Hose or bucket of water
- Vocabulary and/or pictures

DIRECTIONS

1. Pre-teach targeted vocabulary.

2. Discuss the uses of a bird bath, clean water, and dirty water (view pictures, books, Internet pictures, and so on).

3. Transition outdoors.

4. Verbally direct and demonstrate the process of emptying, cleaning, and filling the bird bath. The use of visual schedules, pictures, and/or ordinal numbers as students work may help them understand the process of emptying, cleaning, and filling the bird bath.

5. Direct one student to empty the bird bath.

6. Have students wash the inside, sides and bottom of the bird bath with the sponge and water.

7. Have a student rinse out the dirt and dirty water.

8. Have students take turns filling the bird bath with clean water.*

9. Direct students to restore the work area.

*Students are encouraged in using the hose independently, turning water on and off, determining the water level of the bird bath, communicating effectively with peers or adults to request materials, and discussing each task.

CLEAN SWEEP

MATERIALS
- Brooms
- Gloves (if needed)
- Trash can and recycle bin

DIRECTIONS
1. Pre-teach targeted vocabulary.
2. Discuss the importance of having clean walkways and play areas.
3. Give students a broom.*
4. Transition to the outdoor learning environment.
5. Provide each student with an opportunity to sweep an area. Attend to cleanliness, type of material being swept, trash, debris, and so on.
6. Dispose of trash, debris, recyclables, and the like as appropriate.
7. Share thoughts and ideas about the work (e.g., Was it easy or hard? Are students proud of their accomplishments?).
8. Transition inside.
9. Return broom(s).

*Each student may have a broom, or they may share a broom.

FILL THE BIRD BATH

MATERIALS
- Hose
- Buckets of water
- Pitchers of water
- Vocabulary and/or pictures

DIRECTIONS
1. Pre-teach targeted vocabulary.
2. Discuss the uses of a bird bath, clean water, and dirty water (view pictures, books, Internet pictures, and so on).
3. Transition outdoors.
4. Demonstrate the process of cleaning the bird bath. (Empty bird bath and then fill the bird bath.) The use visual schedules, pictures, and/or ordinal numbers as students work may help to understand the process of emptying, cleaning, and filling the bird bath.
5. Have a student empty the bird bath.
6. Direct students to rinse out dirt and dirty water.
7. Have students take turns filling the bird bath with clean water.*
8. Direct students to restore the work area.
9. Transition inside.

*Encourage students to use the hose independently by turning water on and off, determine the water level in the bird bath, and communicate effectively with peers or adults.

FILL THE BIRD FEEDER

MATERIALS
- Birdseed
- Bird feeders
- Scoop
- Vocabulary and/or pictures

DIRECTIONS
1. Pre-teach targeted vocabulary.
2. Transition from classroom to bird feeder station.
3. Identify the different types of birdseed.
4. Explore the birdseed with the senses—touch, smell, and vision—then discuss students' perceptions, thoughts, and ideas.
5. Scoop birdseed into the bird feeder until the feeder is full.
6. Hang the bird feeder.
7. Transition to the classroom.

GARDEN JOURNAL COVER

MATERIALS
- Pictures of a garden, garden tools, and plants for cutting
- Construction paper
- Crayons, markers, colored pencils
- Glue
- Scissors
- Pencil

DIRECTIONS
1. Pre-teach targeted vocabulary.
2. Discuss the pictures of the garden, garden tools, and plants.
3. Have students select a piece of construction paper.
4. Direct students to fold construction paper in half to make a book.
5. Have each student write his or her name on the back of the construction paper book.
6. Monitor students as they cut out the pictures of the garden, garden tools, and plants.
7. Have students glue the pictures onto the front of the garden books.
8. Have each student decorate the front, insides, and back of his or her book, if desired, with crayons, markers, or colored pencils.
9. Direct students to restore the work area.

GARDEN JOURNAL OBSERVATIONS AND DRAWINGS

MATERIALS
- Garden journal cover
- Drawing paper
- Writing paper
- Pencil
- Crayons, markers, colored pencils
- Magnifying glass
- Ruler
- Stapler

DIRECTIONS
1. Pre-teach targeted vocabulary.
2. Gather the garden journals and materials; then transition to the outdoor learning area.
3. Discuss the characteristics of the plants, insects, animals, reptiles, and other living things that can be observed at this time.
4. Have each student choose an item to observe (students may choose to use rulers or magnifying glasses).
5. Direct each student to gather one piece of drawing paper, one piece of writing paper, a pencil, and crayons, markers, or colored pencils.
6. Direct each student to place his or her name and the date on each piece of paper.
7. Encourage students to draw and color their observations with crayons, markers, pencils, and/or colored pencils on the drawing paper.
8. Direct students to write about their observations and include colors, sizes, and other details.
9. Staple the two pages together and place them into the garden journals.*
10. Direct students to restore work area and transition indoors.

*Pages can be added to the journal throughout the year.

HARVEST TIME

MATERIALS
- Student scissors
- Tray
- Storage bag for harvested items
- Vocabulary and/or pictures

DIRECTIONS
1. Pre-teach targeted vocabulary.
2. Review and discuss with students the garden plants and plant changes.
3. Have students use the scissors to clip off herbs or vegetables or pick them by hand.
4. Give students an opportunity to observe, smell, and touch the herbs or vegetables and to discuss their perceptions, thoughts, and ideas.
5. Direct students to place the harvested items on a tray.
6. Instruct students to wash the harvested items and to place them in a storage bag to take home or to use for a classroom cooking activity.

MINI METEOROLOGIST

MATERIALS
- A variety of weather instruments previously placed outdoors (e.g., weather vane, outdoor thermometer, rain gage, or wind vane)
- Student garden journal (pictures of weather instruments can be added to the journal for an organized recording of data)
- Bag of pencils

DIRECTIONS
1. Pre-teach targeted vocabulary (instruments and their functions).
2. Encourage students to make predictions about the day's weather data.
3. Transition outdoors to designated learning environment.
4. Direct students, one at a time, to each instrument.
5. Have students record data from each instrument into their garden journals.
6. Form a circle and have reflective discussion on each student's predictions and data collected.
7. Transition indoors.

PICK UP TRASH AND RECYCLABLES

MATERIALS
- Trash bags
- Recycle bin
- Gloves (if needed)
- Vocabulary and/or pictures

DIRECTIONS
1. Pre-teach targeted vocabulary.
2. Discuss differences in trash and recyclable items.
3. Give the group of students one bag for collecting trash and one bag for collecting recyclable materials.
4. Transition to the outdoor learning environment.
5. Direct each student to collect a specified number of trash and/or recyclable items and to place them in the appropriate bags.
6. Have students place trash in trash receptacle and recyclables in the recycle bin.

PLANTING SEEDS

This activity may be performed indoors or outdoors.

MATERIALS
- Seeds of herbs and/or vegetables
- Soil
- Plant containers
- Trowel(s) (1 trowel per 3 students)
- Water
- Watering can
- A paper towel or a paper plate

DIRECTIONS
1. Pre-teach targeted vocabulary.
2. Open a variety of seed packets and spread seeds on the paper towel or paper plate.
3. Examine and discuss the seeds, soil, trowel, planting container, and watering can.
4. Use the trowel to scoop soil into the container(s), filling each container almost to the top.
5. Use a finger to poke a hole into the soil.
6. Have students choose which seed(s) they would like to plant, and have them place their seed(s) into the hole(s) in the soil.
7. Direct students to use the trowel or a hand to cover the seed and fill the hole with soil.
8. Have students fill the watering can with water.
9. Direct students to water the seeds.
10. Have students place the seed-filled containers by a window or light.
11. Direct students to restore the work area.
12. Water the seeds regularly as directed by the seed packet.
13. Observe the plants as they sprout and grow.

SOIL PREPARATION FOR PLANTING

This activity may be performed indoors or outdoors. If it is performed inside, a broom and dustpan may be needed for cleanup.

MATERIALS
- Soil
- Plant containers
- Trowel(s)

DIRECTIONS
1. Pre-teach targeted vocabulary.
2. Explore the soil with the senses—touch, smell, and vision—then discuss students' perceptions, thoughts, and ideas.
3. Examine and discuss the characteristics and importance of using the soil, trowel, and planting containers.
4. Use the trowel to scoop soil into the container; fill container almost to the top.
5. Direct students to restore the work area.

WATER THE GARDEN

MATERIALS
- Watering can(s)*
- Access to outside water spigot
- Potted plants
- Garden plot
- Tree bags
- Vocabulary words and pictures

DIRECTIONS
1. Pre-teach targeted vocabulary.
2. Have the students discuss the importance of water and of watering plants.
3. Demonstrate how to turn the water spigot on and off.
4. Demonstrate how to hold the hose and fill the watering can. (A spray nozzle is beneficial to conserve water and to reinforce hand strength).
5. Direct a student to turn on the water.
6. Allow students to fill their watering cans and to transport them to identified plants and trees.
7. Encourage students to water identified plants and trees.
8. Direct the last user to turn off the water.
9. Direct students to restore the work area.

*A plastic drink pitcher works well for younger students. Each student may have his/her own pitcher or share to encourage taking turns and waiting.

WEED THE GARDEN

MATERIALS
- Gloves as necessary
- Pictures of plants and weeds to sort
- Compost container
- Vocabulary words and pictures

DIRECTIONS
1. Pre-teach targeted vocabulary.
2. Discuss the question: What is a weed?
3. Have students look at a variety of pictures of weeds and preferred plants and then sort pictures into the preferred plant or weed category.
4. Encourage students to observe weeds and plants in the outdoor learning environment.
5. Demonstrate how to pull weeds (grasp the base of stalks and pull out).
6. Allow students to grasp and pull weeds. Repeat until all weeds have been removed.
7. Place removed weeds in a compost container or pile.
8. Direct students to restore the work area.
9. Transition to the classroom.

Autumn Activities

ACORN PAINTING

This activity can be divided into a nature walk and a painting activity. Once acorns have been collected, the painting activity may be carried out on the same day or on a different day.

MATERIALS
- Paint in a variety of colors (glitter paint is a nice addition)
- Boxes, box tops, or cake pans
- Paper
- Sandwich bags
- Pencils or pens
- Vocabulary and/or pictures

DIRECTIONS
1. Pre-teach targeted vocabulary.
2. Give each student a sandwich bag for collecting acorns.
3. Transition to the outdoor learning environment.
4. Direct each student to collect a specified number of acorns and place them in his/her sandwich bag.
5. Transition to next work station; this may be indoors or outdoors.
6. Direct students to write their names on their papers before painting.
7. Place the paper into the boxes, box tops, or cake pans.
8. Add several different colors of paint in quarter size drops to the paper.
9. Add acorns to the box.
10. Tilt or shake the box to move the acorns through the paint and across the paper (left, right, front, back).
11. Remove painted paper from the box and place in a secure location to dry.
12. Direct students to restore the work area.

AUTUMN COLOR QUEST

MATERIALS
- A variety of paint color sample cards (fabric color swatches, wrapping paper swatches, construction paper swatches, crayons, markers, or paint in autumn colors can be used)
- A bag to hold colored items

DIRECTIONS
1. Pre-teach targeted vocabulary.
2. Transition outdoors to designated outdoor learning environment.
3. Have each student obtain a color sample from the bag.
4. Have students match the color samples to various environmental items (e.g., yellow swatch to yellow leaf).
5. Encourage students to exchange colors with one another and repeat step 4 with each color exchange.
6. Transition indoors to designated learning environment.

Items can be collected to assemble an autumn color quest collage.

AUTUMN POTPOURRI 1

MATERIALS
- One small or large orange, depending on student age and fine motor needs
- Paper towels
- Microwave or dehydrator (if one is available)

DIRECTIONS
1. Pre-teach targeted vocabulary.
2. Discuss characteristics of the orange (color, shape, food category, grows on tree, texture, and smell).
3. Peel the fruit.
   a. If using paper towels and microwave, follow steps 4, 5, and 7.
   b. If using a dehydrator, skip to step 6.
4. Set several paper towels on a microwave-safe plate. Place orange peels on the paper towels. Cover the orange peels with three or four layers of paper towels. Microwave at fifty percent for five minutes, rotating halfway through if the microwave does not have a carousel.
5. Remove peels and store in a cool, dry place for two to three days, until completely dry.
6. Place orange peels on dehydrator tray. Dehydrate according to the instructions for the dehydrator.
7. Allow students to eat orange sections, take to compost bin/pile, or toss into wood line for natural decomposition or animal and insect consumption.

AUTUMN POTPOURRI 2

MATERIALS
- Whole spices (cinnamon, nutmeg, and cloves)
- Small hammer
- Sandwich bag

DIRECTIONS
1. Pre-teach targeted vocabulary.
2. Have students open spice containers and remove spices.
3. Encourage students to examine the different spices and to discuss their characteristics (size, shape, smell, texture, and the like).
4. Direct students to place the spices inside sturdy sandwich bags and to seal them.
5. Instruct students to use the hammer to smash the spices into small pieces, thereby breaking up the spices to release the fragrant oils.
6. Store spices in the sandwich bag until potpourri assembly.

AUTUMN POTPOURRI 3

MATERIALS
- Bark, twigs
- Acorns
- Tree nuts (allergy permitting)
- Pinecones
- Garden herbs
- Dried orange peels
- Dried spices (cinnamon, nutmeg, and cloves)
- Small sandwich bags
- Large food storage bags or covered bowls
- Measuring cups
- Large spoons

DIRECTIONS
1. Pre-teach targeted vocabulary.
2. Go on a nature walk. Take several sandwich bags to collect interesting nature items to toss in the potpourri mix. Include acorns and other tree nuts, bark, interesting twigs, and pinecones. Add fresh or dried herbs from an herb garden.
3. Measure out ten cups of fresh natural materials and two cups of the spices and place them into the large bowl or storage bag. Add all orange peels and mix all ingredients thoroughly, but gently, with hands or two large spoons.
4. Store the mixture in one or more large storage bags for at least two weeks. Shake the mixture gently once every day.
5. Pour the potpourri into a bowl and display it in the desired location.

The potpourri can also be used as a gift if it is wrapped or placed in a decorative storage container.

FALL WINDOW DECORATIONS

MATERIALS
- Resealable sandwich-sized bags
- Clear adhesive-backed paper
- Leaves in a variety of shapes, sizes, and colors
- String or yarn
- Tape or hole punch

DIRECTIONS
1. Pre-teach targeted vocabulary.
2. Transition outdoors to designated outdoor learning environment.
3. Give each student a bag to collect items and carry during their walk.
4. Have students collect leaves in a variety of shapes, sizes, and colors.
5. Encourage students to identify items, colors, and shapes in their bags.
6. Include discussions on:
    a. Identification of sensory aspects of students' finds (heavy or light? smooth or rough? big or little? smell or no smell?).
    b. The function of leaves for animals (e.g., shade, nesting material, food resource, life cycles, habitat).
    c. The function that leaves serve for plants and trees (photosynthesis, production of oxygen, and absorption of carbon dioxide).
7. Transition into the classroom.
8. Have students retrieve items from their bags and place items on the clear adhesive side of the paper.
9. Cover the items with the clear adhesive side of the paper.
10. Cut out the cluster of items in a leaf shape.
11. Attach yarn or string to leaf shape with tape, or use hole punch on shape and tie yarn or string through the hole.
12. Hang shape in window with yarn or string, or tape directly to window.

LEAF RUBBINGS

MATERIALS
- A variety of leaves
- A variety of fall-colored crayons
- White paper
- Clipboards (if working outside)

DIRECTIONS
1. Pre-teach targeted vocabulary.
2. Transition outdoors to designated outdoor learning environment.
3. Look at and collect a variety of leaves.
4. Identify each leaf by color, size, and shape then label the leaf parts (vein, stem, etc.).
5. Discuss leaf and leaf parts (veins, stem, etc.), articulate ideas, match big and small leaves, match colors, match shapes, and discuss textures, and similarities/differences).

The remaining activity may take place indoors or outdoors.

6. Have each student select a leaf, a white piece of paper, and a clipboard, if needed, for outdoor activity.
7. Have each student select a crayon and remove paper from the crayon.
8. Have students place a leaf under a piece of white paper.
9. Have students press paper down and hold the leaf and the paper in place (encourage bilateral hand use).
10. Direct students to use the side of the crayon and rub the crayon across leaves; rub in a lateral or horizontal motion to highlight the edges, veins, and stem of the leaves.
11. Direct students to remove the white paper from the leaves.
12. Have students return leaves.
13. Repeat as desired.

PASS THE PUMPKIN

MATERIAL
- One small pumpkin

DIRECTIONS
1. Pre-teach targeted vocabulary.

2. Transition outdoors in a small group.

3. Discuss, compare, and contrast the characteristics of pumpkins (shape, size, smell, texture, etc.).

4. Direct students to sit in a circle to prepare to pass the pumpkin.

5. Begin passing the pumpkin when the teacher calls, "Go." When the teacher calls, "Stop," the students should immediately stop passing the pumpkin. The person holding the pumpkin when "stop" is called is "in the pumpkin patch" and sits inside the circle. The game continues until only one student is left. This student is declared the "Harvest Pumpkin."

6. Have the "Harvest Pumpkin" give characteristics describing how he or she would appear as a pumpkin (big/little, round/elongated, rough/smooth).

7. Transition indoors.

SPIDER SNACK

MATERIALS
- Pretzel sticks (long for long legs or broken for short legs)
- Candy corn (short legs)
- Shoelace licorice (red or black, for long or short legs)
- Round cream-filled sandwich cookies (white or black, for body)
- Paper plates
- Vocabulary and/or pictures (real spiders)

DIRECTIONS
1. Pre-teach targeted vocabulary.
2. Discuss spiders (e.g., how many legs they have, what they eat).
3. Have students wash hands thoroughly prior to handling food.
4. Use appropriate communication and language to pass items to peers and request items from peers.
5. Have each student retrieve a paper plate.
6. Have students identify which type of spider legs (pretzels, candy corn, or licorice) to use and which length (long or short) to use.
7. Have students count out eight spider legs and place them on their plates.
8. Direct each student to gather a body and place it on his or her plate.
9. Encourage students to remove cookie tops by twisting gently.
10. Monitor students' placement of the legs in the cream filling of the cookie similar to that of a real spider (four on each side of the body). Talk about right and left and symmetry.
11. Have each student show his or her spider snack creation to group.
12. Encourage students to eat and enjoy their spider snacks; engage in conversation and feedback during snack time.
13. Direct students to restore the work area.

Some students may have known allergies and be on special diets.

SPIDER WEB

MATERIALS
- White yarn
- Scissors
- Paper plates
- Black crayons
- Rulers
- Tape
- Plastic spiders
- Pictures of real spiders/vocabulary

DIRECTIONS
1. Pre-teach targeted vocabulary.
2. Discuss spiders (e.g., how many legs they have, what they eat).
3. Encourage students to use appropriate communication and language to pass items to peers and request items from peers.
4. Have each student retrieve a paper plate and a black crayon.
5. Direct students to color one side of the paper plates black.
6. Instruct students to snip six notches around the diameter of the plate.
7. Encourage students to request the white yarn.
8. Have each student measure and cut a six-foot piece of yarn.
9. Direct students to tape one end of the yarn to the back of the plates (the white sides).
10. Support students in looping the yarn around the paper plate into the notches, crossing the plate diagonally to each notch.
11. Have students tape remaining yarn to the back of the plates.
12. Have students request the plastic spiders.
13. Have each student measure and cut a twelve-inch piece of yarn.

14. Facilitate each student's tying of one end of the yarn around the plastic spider and the opposite end of the yarn to the spider web.

15. Discuss spider webs and spiders.

16. Direct students to restore the work area.

Winter Activities

EVERGREEN NEEDLE PAINTING

MATERIALS
- Paint
- Paint tray
- Art paper
- Scissors
- Vocabulary and/or pictures

DIRECTIONS
1. Pre-teach targeted vocabulary.
2. Review and discuss evergreen trees.
3. Transition to the outdoor learning environment.
4. Identify evergreen trees.
5. Use scissors to clip needle clusters as appropriate.
6. Explore the freshly clipped needle clusters and discuss the students' perceptions, thoughts, and ideas about the clusters.
7. Transition to the classroom or an outdoor work area.
8. Have students dip needle clusters into paint.
9. Instruct students to use paint-covered needles to paint designs on the paper.
10. Direct students to restore work area.

GROUNDHOG DAY

MATERIALS
- Picture of a real groundhog and/or one in fiction and nonfiction storybook for discussion
- Wooden craft sticks
- Brown crayons
- Glue
- Scissors
- Pencils
- Vocabulary and/or pictures

DIRECTIONS
1. Pre-teach targeted vocabulary.
2. Discuss a groundhog and the significance of Groundhog Day. Look at pictures of groundhogs. Talk about winter hibernation. Look at pictures of a variety of shadows. Make shadows as appropriate for the individual students' learning levels, and predict if the groundhog will see his shadow.
3. Direct students to write their names on craft sticks.
4. Have students use a brown crayon to color line-drawn pictures of a groundhog.
5. Supervise as students cut out their groundhog pictures.
6. Direct students to glue their groundhog pictures onto the craft sticks.
7. Have each student take their groundhog that is attached to the stick, outside to the school garden and push the craft stick into the ground several inches until stable.
8. Observe if the groundhog makes a shadow and make a spring prediction.

MAKE A BIRD FEEDER

MATERIALS
- Yarn or string
- Scissors
- Pinecones, toilet paper rolls, paper towel rolls
- Cream cheese*
- Birdseed
- Box or cake pan
- Spoon (optional), to spread cream cheese
- Vocabulary and/or pictures

This activity may be carried out inside the classroom or in the outdoor learning environment. It can be an individual or group project.

DIRECTIONS
1. Pre-teach targeted vocabulary.
2. Pour or scoop birdseed into a cake pan or box.
3. Cover pinecone with cream cheese by rolling pinecone in block of cream cheese or using spoon to spread the cream cheese on pinecone.
4. Cover cream cheese pinecone with birdseed; place cream cheese-covered pinecone into the cake pan or box. Roll pinecone in the birdseed by rolling it in the box, or pour birdseed over pinecone.
5. Choose colored yarn. Use scissors to cut length of yarn, and tie a knot (practice tying) Tie a piece of string or yarn to the very top of the pinecone. Loop the string under the topmost "leaves" of the pinecone and tie a knot in the top.
6. Hang the bird feeder on a tree branch in the yard and watch the birds gather. Have students make observations of the birds that come to their feeders.

*For easier spreading, the block of cream cheese should be removed from the refrigerator 30 minutes prior to use.

MAKE A CARDINAL

MATERIALS
- Pictures of cardinals for discussion
- Outline of a cardinal (print free from the Internet)
- Red and brown craft feathers
- Crayons
- Glue
- Scissors
- Pencils
- Vocabulary and/or pictures

DIRECTIONS
1. Pre-teach targeted vocabulary.
2. Discuss cardinals; discuss the different colors of the male and female; look at pictures of cardinals; and talk about what they eat and where they live.
3. Direct students to write their names on the cardinal outline handout.
4. Have students color the outlines, using appropriate crayon colors to color the picture, attending to the details of the picture (branches, leaves, evergreen needles, sky, and so on).
5. Glue the feathers to the cardinal, using the appropriate colored feathers.
6. Take finished picture to a secure location to dry.
7. Direct students to restore the work area.
8. Observe to see if there are cardinals in the outdoor learning area.

Shape Walk

MATERIALS
- A variety of handheld shapes (i.e. circle, square, triangle, etc.)
- A bag to hold items
- Vocabulary and/or pictures

DIRECTIONS
1. Pre-teach targeted vocabulary.
2. Transition outdoors to designated learning environment.
3. Have students obtain shape samples from the bag.
4. Encourage students to find a matching shape while comparing its shape to various environmental items (e.g., circle to flowerpot opening).
5. Discuss what makes a square a square, what makes a circle a circle, etc.
6. Encourage students to exchange shapes with one another and repeat steps 4 and 5.
7. Return all shapes to the bag.
8. Transition indoors.

SNOWMAN TREATS

MATERIALS
- Pretzel sticks (one per student)
- Medium-sized marshmallows (two per student)
- Gel frosting tube (optional)
- Paper plates or paper towels
- Vocabulary and/or pictures

DIRECTIONS
1. Pre-teach targeted vocabulary.
2. Discuss the characteristics of a snowman (shape, types of clothes, if it is found in winter or summer, and so on).
3. Have students request needed materials from peers or adults (two marshmallows, one pretzel stick) and place the materials on their paper towel or plate.
4. Have students each tear one marshmallow in half.
5. Students will stack the three marshmallows.
6. Have students break pretzel sticks in half.
7. Have students push pretzels into the marshmallows to make arms.
8. If using gel frosting, have the students use it to add eyes, noses, and mouths to their snowmen.
9. Encourage students to eat snowman treats.
10. Direct students to restore the work area.

Some students may have known allergies or be on a special diet.

Squirrel Habitat

MATERIALS
- Pictures of a squirrel and a squirrel's drey from books or the Internet
- Student garden journals
- Bag of pencils and crayons

DIRECTIONS
1. Pre-teach targeted vocabulary.
2. Transition outdoors to designated outdoor learning environment.
3. Encourage students to notice squirrels around the outdoor learning environment.
4. Have students examine the treetops for a squirrel's drey.
5. Discuss the types of trees and the height of trees in which the drey was noticed.
6. Direct students to draw images in their garden journals and write what they observed about squirrels and squirrel habitats.
7. Return drawing and writing tools to the bag.
8. Transition indoors.

Spring Activities

BIRD NEST HELPER BAG

This activity may be performed indoors or outdoors.

MATERIALS
- Mesh bags (fruit or onion bags)

Use any of the following materials, as available:
- Fabric scraps
- Yarn
- String
- Ribbon
- Dried grass
- Spanish moss
- Dog hair, human hair, or horse mane
- Vocabulary and/or pictures

DIRECTIONS
1. Pre-teach targeted vocabulary.
2. Observe and discuss a variety of bird nests (photos of nests, real nests).
3. Discuss the purpose of a nest and materials in a nest.
4. Examine nest-helping materials.
5. Have students take turns placing materials into mesh bags until filled.
6. Hang mesh bags outside for the birds.

Some students may have known allergies.

CAMOUFLAGE CRAZE

MATERIALS
- A variety of colored pipe cleaners pre-hidden in the outdoor learning environment (e.g., green pipe cleaner added to a plant stalk)

DIRECTIONS
1. Pre-teach targeted vocabulary.
2. Transition outdoors to designated learning environment.
3. Direct students to locate the pipe cleaners.
4. Have students discuss the effectiveness of camouflage.
5. Encourage students to name animals that utilize camouflage and why.
6. Transition indoors.

DECIDUOUS TREES AND EVERGREEN TREES

MATERIALS
- A deciduous tree
- An evergreen tree
- Student garden journals
- Bag of pencils and crayons

DIRECTIONS
1. Pre-teach targeted vocabulary.
2. Transition outdoors to designated learning environment.
3. Direct students to locate a deciduous tree.
4. Direct students to locate an evergreen tree.
5. Discuss the differences observed.
6. Encourage students to draw both trees in their garden journals and to record their thoughts about the trees.
7. Direct students to label their drawings with the current season.
8. Collect materials and transition indoors.

Each season, students can visit the same trees and draw and record their observations.

HERB PLANTING

MATERIALS
- Seeds for individual herb varieties
- Soil
- Plant containers
- Trowels
- Water
- Watering can(s)
- Paper towels or paper plates

DIRECTIONS
1. Pre-teach targeted vocabulary.
2. Open a variety of seed packets and spread the seeds on the paper towel or paper plate.
3. Examine and discuss the seeds, soil, trowel, planting container, and watering can.
4. Direct students to use the trowel to scoop soil into the container(s), filling each container almost to the top.
5. Instruct students to use a finger to poke a hole into the soil.
6. Direct students to choose which seed(s) they would like to plant, and have them place the seed(s) into the holes in the soil.
7. Instruct students to use the trowel or a hand to cover the seed and fill the hole with soil.
8. Have student(s) fill the watering can(s) with water.
9. Direct students to water the seeds as directed by the seed packets.
10. Have students place the seed-filled container(s) by a window, by a light, or outside.
11. Direct students to restore the work area.
12. Water the seeds regularly.
13. Observe the herbs as they sprout and grow.

LIVING AND NONLIVING

MATERIALS
- Printed terms: living and nonliving

DIRECTIONS
1. Pre-teach targeted vocabulary (living and nonliving).
2. Transition outdoors to designated learning environment.
3. Direct students to locate an item in the natural environment.
4. Have students state if the item is living or nonliving.
5. Encourage a student to hold the correct term next to the item and to communicate a statement to express his or her opinion (e.g., "I think grass is living because…" or "I think mulch is nonliving because…").
6. Repeat steps 3-5 as activity time permits.
7. Transition indoors.

MOTHER'S DAY LAVENDER POUCH

MATERIALS
- Scissors
- Paper plates or containers
- Fresh lavender from the garden
- Small gift pouches (a pouch with holes works well, or make your own with netting or lace from a fabric store)
- Pens, markers, or pencils
- Tags
- Hole punch
- String or ribbon
- Vocabulary and/or pictures

DIRECTIONS
1. Pre-teach targeted vocabulary.
2. Transition to the outdoor learning environment.
3. Allow students to identify lavender.
4. Provide an opportunity for students to observe, smell, and touch the herb and to discuss their perceptions, thoughts, and ideas.
5. Demonstrate how to handle and cut lavender.
6. Allow students to handle and cut lavender.
7. Place clippings onto the paper plates or into pouches.
8. Have students fill pouches to desired level.
9. Direct students to tie pouches with string or ribbon to make knots or bows, depending on the students' abilities.
10. Encourage students to use hole punch to make holes in the tags.
11. Have students write messages on tags.
12. Direct students to tie the tags to the lavender pouches.
13. Direct students to restore the work area.

NACHOS

MATERIALS

- Fresh tomatoes, scallions, cilantro, lettuce, jalapeño, or other vegetables from the garden
- Corn chips, pita chips, or pretzel chips
- Shredded cheese (optional)
- Salsa (optional)
- Sour cream (optional)
- Paper plates
- Cups
- Spoon for each topping
- Clean scissors
- Vocabulary and/or pictures

DIRECTIONS

1. Pre-teach targeted vocabulary.
2. Discuss nachos, snack foods, salty foods, food with cheese, and so on.
3. Wash hands thoroughly prior to handling food.
4. Have students use appropriate communication and language to pass items and request items with peers.
5. Encourage the proper use of scissors to cut the vegetables into tiny bits and place the bits into cups.
6. Count the selected number of chips, identified by the teacher, and place them on plates.
7. Have the students spoon each ingredient onto the chips.
8. Encourage students to eat nachos.
9. Engage in conversation and feedback during snack time.

Some students may have known allergies and be on a special diet.

NEAR AND FAR

MATERIALS
- A distant tree
- A near tree
- Student garden journals
- Bag of pencils and crayons

DIRECTIONS
1. Pre-teach targeted vocabulary.
2. Transition outdoors to designated learning environment.
3. Direct students to locate a nearby tree.
4. Direct students to identify a faraway tree.
5. Discuss the differences observed.
6. Encourage students to draw both trees in their garden journals and record their thoughts about them.
7. Collect materials.
8. Transition indoors.

SIMPLE MACHINES

MATERIALS
- Pictures of simple machines (lever, wedge, screw, wheel, pulley)
- Bag in which to place pictures
- Clipboard, paper, and pencil

DIRECTIONS
1. Pre-teach targeted vocabulary.
2. Transition outdoors to designated learning environment.
3. Have each student select a picture from the bag.
4. Encourage students to look for examples of simple machines in the environment.
5. Direct one student to record examples of items the students discovered (e.g., a ramp is a wedge).
6. Transition indoors.

SPRING COLOR QUEST

MATERIALS
- A variety of paint color sample cards (fabric color swatches, wrapping paper swatches, construction paper swatches, crayons, markers, and paint in spring colors can be used)
- A bag to hold colored items

DIRECTIONS
1. Pre-teach targeted vocabulary.
2. Transition outdoors to designated outdoor learning environment.
3. Have each student obtain a color sample.
4. Encourage students to match their color samples to various environmental items (e.g., green swatch to green grass).
5. Foster students' exchange of colors with one another.
6. Repeat steps 3-5 as activity time permits.
7. Transition indoors.

Items can be collected to assemble a spring color quest collage.

Summer Activities

ANT HABITATS

MATERIALS
- Pictures of ant nests from books or the Internet
- Magnifying glass
- Garden journals
- Bag of pencils and crayons

DIRECTIONS
1. Pre-teach targeted vocabulary.
2. Transition outdoors to designated learning environment.
3. Encourage students to notice ant nests in the natural environment.
4. Have students observe the nest(s) for activity.
5. Discuss the nest location, the appearance of the ant habitat, and the activity of the ants.
6. Direct students to draw the nest in their garden journals and to write their thoughts from the discussion.
7. Have students return writing tools to the bag.
8. Transition indoors.

CUT AND BUNDLE MINT

This activity can be accomplished outside or inside.

MATERIALS
- String
- Scissors
- Paper plate or container
- Fresh mint from the garden
- Pen, marker, and pencil
- Tags
- Hole punch
- Vocabulary and/or pictures

DIRECTIONS
1. Pre-teach targeted vocabulary.
2. Transition to the outdoor learning environment.
3. Allow students to identify mint.
4. Provide opportunity for students to observe, smell, and touch the herb and to discuss their perceptions, thoughts, and ideas about it.
5. Demonstrate how to handle and cut mint.
6. Allow students to handle and cut mint.
7. Direct students to place clippings on the paper plate or in a container.
8. Have students count out specified number of clippings to bundle.
9. Have students tie string around bundled mint to make knots or bows, depending on the students' abilities.
10. Have students use hole punch to make a hole in the tags.
11. Encourage students to write a message on their tag.
12. Allow students to string their tag and tie it to the mint bundle.
13. Direct students to restore the work area.

JUICE

MATERIALS

- Lemons, limes, and oranges (cut in half prior to this activity)
- Water (bottled, fountain)
- Juicer
- Sweetener
- Spoon
- Cups
- Paper towels
- Vocabulary and/or pictures

DIRECTIONS

1. Pre-teach targeted vocabulary.
2. Discuss the different fruits available (color, taste, uses, and so on).
3. Have students wash hands thoroughly prior to handling food.
4. Encourage students to use appropriate communication and language to pass items and request items with peers.
5. Direct students to retrieve a cup.
6. Have students choose two halves of the same fruit.
7. Have students place half of selected fruit in the juicer (use any type of juicer; make sure there is a container or cup to catch juice).
8. Have students place the other half of the fruit into the juicer and repeat.
9. Direct students to pour juice into their cup.
10. Allow students to add water to the juice in the cup until the cup is almost full.
11. Direct students to add sweetener to taste.
12. Encourage students to drink the juice.
13. Engage students in conversation and feedback during snack time.

Some students may have known allergies and be on a special diet.

ME AND MY SHADOW

MATERIALS
- Sidewalk chalk
- Sunlight
- Students in cooperative pairs

DIRECTIONS
1. Pre-teach targeted vocabulary.
2. Assign student partners and transition outdoors to designated learning environment.
3. Encourage students to notice shadows in the natural environment.
4. Have one student in each pair stand in a running position.
5. Encourage the other student in the pair to examine their partner's shadow.
6. Discuss how shadows are made.
7. Direct the student partners not standing still to trace the shadows.
8. Have students label each shadow with the corresponding student's name.
9. Allow each students to make a shadow pose and to trace his or her partner's shadow.
10. Collect chalk.
11. Transition indoors.

SENSES

MATERIALS
- Student garden journals
- Writing and drawing tools

DIRECTIONS
1. Pre-teach targeted vocabulary.
2. Transition outdoors to designated learning environment.
3. Direct students to sit in a circle.
4. Encourage students to notice what they hear, smell, see, feel, and taste.
5. Discuss students' observations and how their senses gathered information about the world around them.
6. Have students complete a garden journal entry.

    Sample entry:
    I hear…
    I smell…
    I see…
    I feel…
    I taste…

7. Collect materials and transition indoors.

SOCK WALK

MATERIALS
- Extra pair of socks per student (white is preferred)
- Magnifying glass(es)
- Pictures of seeds found in the local environment

DIRECTIONS
1. Pre-teach targeted vocabulary.
2. Transition to designated outdoor learning environment.
3. Direct students to put on their extra socks over their existing shoes.
4. Direct students to walk around in a grassy area.
5. Have students sit down and examine the bottom of their socks with a magnifying glass.
6. Encourage students to discuss what they find on their socks.
7. Discuss the various ways in which seeds travel.
8. Remove extra socks. Return any missing footwear, and transition indoors.

TEXTURE WALK

MATERIALS
- Paper swatches
- Student garden journals
- Bag of pencils and crayons

DIRECTIONS
1. Pre-teach targeted vocabulary.
2. Transition to designated outdoor learning environment.
3. Encourage students to notice and feel textures in the natural environment.
4. Have students make rubbings of the textures they find using paper swatches and pencils or crayons.
5. Direct students to label the rubbings (e.g., tree bark, sidewalk).
6. Have students return drawing and writing tools to the bag.
7. Direct students to place their texture rubbings in their garden journals.
8. Transition indoors.

Garden Leisure Activities

NATURE WALK

A nature walk may be taken during any season. Items may be individualized to a specific location.

MATERIALS
- Photographs of items that students may encounter during the walk (e.g., leaves, trees, animals, sky, flowers, plants, stream, acorns, rocks, butterfly, insects)
- Printed words or statements describing above items that students may encounter during the walk

DIRECTIONS
1. Pre-teach targeted vocabulary words.
2. Transition to designated outdoor learning environment.
3. Participate in a leisurely walk while observing, identifying, and discussing the environment and target vocabulary.
4. Transition into the classroom.

SCAVENGER HUNT

MATERIALS

- Resealable sandwich-sized bags
- Optional scavenger hunt items as a sample: leaf, acorn, twig, rock, pinecone, flower, berry, evergreen needle clipping (for demonstration purposes)
- Item list (text or picture lists as appropriate for the students)
- Writing tools

DIRECTIONS

1. Pre-teach targeted vocabulary words.
2. Give each student a list of items to locate, a bag, and a writing tool.
3. Transition to designated outdoor learning environment.
4. Have students collect items on the list and place them in the bags.
5. Have students mark off collected items from their lists.
6. After collecting items, engage students in a discussions on:
    a. Identifying sensory aspects of their finds (e.g., heavy or light? smooth or rough? big or little? smell or no smell?).
    b. The functions that the items serve for animals (e.g., shade, nesting material, food resource, part of life cycles, habitat).
    c. The functions that items serve for plants and trees (e.g., photosynthesis, production of oxygen/absorption of carbon cioxide).
7. Return items to the natural environment.
8. Transition to the classroom.

STEPPING STONE STOMP

For this activity, a previously established stepping stone path can be used if available or a path can be created.

MATERIALS

- Stepping stones or materials to create a path
- Specific activity/directions (e.g., hop on both feet following the path to the end, alternate hops on the right foot, then the left foot following the path to the end)
- Photographs, written directions, or verbal directions as appropriate for students
- Shoes or barefoot option as appropriate for sensory experiences

DIRECTIONS

Previously established path:

1. Pre-teach targeted vocabulary.
2. Transition to designated outdoor learning environment.
3. Direct students to form a line and wait for instructions.
4. Have students engage in activity as directed.
5. Include in post-activity discussion:
    a. Identification of sensory aspects of the stones (e.g., Were the stones heavy or light? Smooth or rough? What did they feel like on students' feet?).
    b. Reflection on fun aspects and challenges of the stepping stone stomp.
6. Collect items.
7. Return to the classroom.

Create a path:

1. Pre-teach targeted vocabulary.
2. Transition to designated outdoor learning environment.
3. Direct students to develop their own "stone" pathway using a variety of materials (e.g., newspaper, floor tiles, rubber pot holders, hula hoops, carpet squares, and construction paper).
4. Follow steps 4–7 from above.

WATER ART

MATERIALS

- Small container(s) to hold water (Students may have their own water containers or share to encourage turn-taking and waiting.)
- Outside water spigot
- Sidewalk
- Paint brushes and paint rollers
- Vocabulary words and pictures

DIRECTIONS

1. Pre-teach targeted vocabulary.
2. Discuss the importance of water conservation.
3. Demonstrate how to turn on/off water spigot.
4. Demonstrate how to hold the hose and fill the water container (a spray nozzle is beneficial to conserve water and to reinforce students' hand strength).
5. Permit students to turn on water.
6. Allow students to fill their water containers and to transport them to a sidewalk area.
7. Have the last student turn off water.
8. Direct students to select a paintbrush or roller.
9. Have students use water as paint to draw freely or draw/copy picture cards or shapes on the sidewalk.
10. Direct students to restore the work area.

WATER GAME 1

Water Balloon Catch

MATERIALS
- Balloons
- Outside water spigot and hose
- Vocabulary words and pictures

DIRECTIONS
1. Pre-teach targeted vocabulary.
2. Discuss the importance of water conservation.
3. Demonstrate how to turn on/off water spigot.
4. Demonstrate how to hold the hose and fill the water container (a spray nozzle is beneficial to conserve water and to reinforce students' hand strength).
5. Have a student turn on water.
6. Direct students to fill the balloons with water.*
7. Have the last student turn off the water.
8. Permit students to tie balloons independently or to ask for assistance.
9. Gather balloons and transition to the game area.
10. Have students throw and catch the balloons (trying to keep balloons intact).
11. Direct students to restore the work area (pick up balloon bits as needed).

*Students can make choices as to how they fill the balloons if provided with a variety of items (e.g., squeeze bottle, funnel, or turkey basting tool).

Students may need sunscreen.

WATER GAME 2

Fill the Bucket

This water game may be played as a team or as an individual effort, pending number of students.

MATERIALS

- Sponges
- Large bucket(s) or container(s)
- Outside water spigot and hose
- Timer
- Vocabulary words and pictures

DIRECTIONS

1. Pre-teach targeted vocabulary.
2. Discuss the importance of water conservation.
3. Demonstrate how to turn on/off water spigot.
4. Demonstrate how to hold the hose and fill the water container (a spray nozzle is beneficial to conserve water and to reinforce students' hand strength).
5. Have a student turn on the water.
6. Allow students to fill container(s) with water.
7. Have the last user turn off water.
8. Have student(s) place empty bucket(s)/container(s) on one end of the play space.
9. Direct students to place water-filled bucket(s)/container(s) opposite the empty bucket(s)/container(s); distance is determined by teacher.
10. Allow students to place sponges in the bucket of water (sponges absorb water).
11. Encourage students to remove the sponges full of water and relay them to the empty buckets.
12. Encourage students to squeeze out the water from the sponges into the empty container.
13. Repeat the process until time has expired.
14. Direct students to restore the work area.

Students may need sunscreen.

WATER GAME 3

Water Nozzle Bull's-Eye

This water game may be played as a team or as an individual effort, depending on number of students.

MATERIALS
- Outside water spigot and hose with a nozzle
- Spray bottles, squeeze bottles, and/or pump bottles*
- Target (e.g., a washcloth, shower curtain, shaving cream, student-made target)
- Vocabulary words and pictures

DIRECTIONS
1. Pre-teach targeted vocabulary.
2. Discuss the importance of water conservation.
3. Demonstrate how to turn on/off water spigot.
4. Demonstrate how to hold the hose and fill the water container (a spray nozzle is beneficial to conserve water and to reinforce students' hand strength).
5. Have a student turn on water.
6. Allow students to fill container(s) with water.
7. Designate a student to turn off the water.
8. Place target(s).
9. Have students stand in a determined location; distance is determined by teacher.
10. Encourage students to manipulate water bottles so that the water is aimed at and hitting the bull's-eye.
11. Direct students to restore the work area.

*The mechanics required to use a spray bottle imitate scissor use, a squeeze bottle facilitates use of hand strength, and a pump bottle facilitates isolated finger movement and strength.

Students may need sunscreen.

Appendix

Student Vocabulary

Dictionary definitions are provided for discussion. Students should be encouraged to formulate their own definitions and draw pictures to support their comprehesion and learning.

Acorn	the fruit or nut of an oak tree
Acorns	more than one acorn
Air	a mixture of nitrogen, oxygen, and minute amounts of other gases that surrounds the earth and forms its atmosphere
All spice	the dried, unripe berries of an aromatic tropical American tree, used whole or ground
Animal	living organism with independent movement
Animals	more than one animal
Ant	an insect with a complex social organization and various castes performing special duties
Ants	more than one ant
Ate	past tense of eat
Bad	failing to reach an acceptable standard
Bark	the tough exterior covering of a woody root or stem
Bee	an insect that differs from the related wasps especially in the heavier hairier body and in having sucking as well as chewing mouthparts, that feed on pollen and nectar, and that store both and often also honey
Bees	more than one bee
Big	large or great in dimensions; bulky
Bird	a feathered vertebrate
Bird bath	an ornamental basin set up for birds to bathe in
Bird feeder	a device or apparatus for supplying food
Bird feeders	more than one bird feeder
Bird house	an artificial nesting site for birds
Bird houses	more than one bird house
Birds	more than one bird
Bitter	being or inducing the one of the four basic taste sensations that is peculiarly acrid; astringent
Black	very dark in color
Blow	the wind or air in motion
Blows	to create a current of moving air by breathing
Blue bird	any of three small North American thrushes
Blue birds	more than one blue bird
Blue jay	crested bright blue North American jay
Blue jays	more than one blue jay
Boulder	a detached and rounded or much-worn mass of rock

Boulders	more than one boulder
Branch	a natural subdivision of a plant stem or tree
Branches	parts of a tree that grow out from the trunk
Breeze	a light gentle wind
Breezy	windy
Bridge	a structure built over something (such as a river) so that people or vehicles can get across
Bridges	more than one bridge
Brown	a tertiary color with a yellowish or reddish hue
Bud	a small lateral or terminal protuberance on the stem of a plant that may develop into a flower, leaf, or shoot
Buds	more than one bud
Bug	an insect or other creeping or crawling invertebrate (as a spider or centipede)
Bugs	more than one insect
Bush	a low, densely branched shrub
Bushes	more than one bush
Butterflies	more than one butterfly
Butterfly	a kind of insect that has a long, thin body and brightly colored wings and that flies mostly during the day
Cardinal	a crested finch
Cardinals	more than one cardinal
Caterpillar	the elongated wormlike larva of a butterfly or moth
Caterpillars	more than one caterpillar
Chilly	noticeably cold
Cinnamon	an aromatic spice prepared from the dried inner bark of a cinnamon tree
Cinnamon stick	sweet spice made from the bark of an Asian tree and used in cooking and baking
Clay	an earthy material that is plastic when moist but hard when fired, that is composed mainly of fine particles of hydrous aluminum silicates and other minerals
Clean	free from dirt or pollution
Clean up	an act or instance of cleaning
Close	to draw near
Closer	nearer
Closest	nearest in space
Cloudy	overcast
Cloves	the dried flower bud of a tropical tree
Cold	having or being a temperature that is uncomfortably low for humans
Colder	a condition of lower temperature
Coldest	having a very low temperature
Color	a phenomenon of light

Compost	a mixture that consists largely of decayed organic matter and that is used for fertilizing and conditioning land
Container	a receptacle (as a box or jar) for holding goods
Containers	more than one container
Cover	to place something over or upon
Creek	a natural stream of water normally smaller than and often tributary to a river
Cut	to divide with a sharp-edged instrument
Dark	devoid or partially devoid of light
Darker	having very little or no light
Darkest	reflecting little light
Dead	deprived of life: no longer living
Decompose	to break up into constituent parts by or as if by a chemical process: decay, rot
Dehydrate	to remove water from
Die	to cease functioning
Dig	to break up, turn, or loosen (as earth) with an implement
Dirt	loose or packed soil or sand: earth
Dried	free or relatively free from a liquid, especially water
Dry	devoid of natural moisture
Eat	to take in through the mouth as food: ingest, chew, and swallow in turn
Edible	fit to be eaten
Environment	the circumstances, objects, or conditions by which one is surrounded
Fall	the season when leaves fall from trees: autumn
Finch	any of several hundred species of small, conical-billed, seed-eating songbirds
Finches	more than one finch
Flower	the part of a seed plant that normally bears reproductive organs: blossom
Flower bed	an area where flowers are planted
Flower pot	a pot in which to grow plants
Flowers	more than one flower
Fly	a winged insect
Flying	moving or able to move in the air
Food	material consisting of protein, carbohydrate, and fat consumed by an organism to sustain growth, repair, perform vital processes, and furnish energy
Fruit	the usually edible reproductive body of a seed plant; especially one having a sweet pulp
Garbage	discarded or useless material
Garden	a plot of ground where trees, herbs, fruits, flowers, or vegetables are cultivated
Garden plot	an area of ground where plants (such as flowers or vegetables) are grown
Gardens	more than one garden
Ginger	a thickened, pungent aromatic rhizome that is used as a spice and sometimes medicinally

Good	suitable; fit
Goods	products that are made or grown to be sold: things for sale
Green	a color of growing foliage
Greener	to become or make a darker shade of green
Greenest	the darkest shade of green
Grow	to spring up and develop to maturity
Growth	the process of developing
Habitat	the place or environment where a plant or animal naturally or normally lives and grows
Hear	to listen to with attention
Hearing	perceiving or apprehending by the ear
Heat	to become or make warm or hot
Herb	a plant or plant part valued for its medicinal, savory, or aromatic qualities
Herbs	more than one herb
Hole	an opening
Hose	a flexible tube for conveying fluids
Hot	having a relatively high temperature
Hotter	having very intense heat
Hottest	being extremely hot
Lavender	Mediterranean mint widely cultivated for its narrow aromatic leaves and spikes of lilac-purple flowers
Leaf	a lateral outgrowth from a plant stem
Leaves	more than one leaf
Light	the form of energy that makes it possible to see things: the brightness produced by the sun, by fire, a lamp, etc.
Little	small in size
Live	to have life
Living	having life
Look	to use one's sight or vision in seeking, searching, examining, watching, etc.
Looking	directing one's eyes at something
Mix	to combine with another
Mixing	combining and becoming one thing that is the same throughout
Mud	soft wet earth
Mulch	a protective covering spread or left on the ground to reduce evaporation, maintain even soil temperature, prevent erosion, control weeds, enrich the soil, or keep fruit (as strawberries) clean
Mulching	covering (the ground, a garden) with mulch
Nature walk	a path through a forest, field, mountain range, etc., that is used for hiking and seeing plants and animals
Non-edible	not to be eaten
Nonliving	never having life

Observation	the act of noticing
Observe	to watch carefully, especially with attention to details or behavior for the purpose of arriving at a judgment
Open	having no enclosing or confining barrier: accessible on all or nearly all sides
Opened	caused (something) to no longer be covered, sealed, or blocked
Opening	a hole or empty space
Orange	any of various small evergreen citrus trees with glossy ovate leaves, hard yellow wood, fragrant white flowers, and fruits that are oranges; a color
Orange peel	the skin of a citrus fruit that is round and has an orange skin
Oranges	more than one orange
Oxygen	a colorless, tasteless, odorless gaseous element that constitutes twenty-one percent of the atmosphere and is found in water, in most rocks and minerals, and in numerous organic compounds
Peel	to strip off an outer layer
Peeled	removed the skin from (a fruit, vegetable, etc.)
Petal	one of the soft, colorful parts of a flower
Petals	more than one petal
Pile	to lay or place in a pile; stack
Piles	more than one pile
Pine	any of coniferous evergreen trees that have slender elongated needles and include some valuable timber trees and ornamentals
Pine cone	a cone of a pine tree
Pine needle	long, thin needle-like growth instead of leaves that stays green throughout the year
Pine needles	the needle-shaped leaves of a pine tree
Plant	to put or set in the ground for growth
Plant	a seedling, herb or other small vegetable growth
Planter	a container in which ornamental plants are grown
Plants	more than one plant
Potpourri	a mixture of flowers, herbs, and spices, usually kept in a jar and used for scent
Pour	to cause to flow in a stream
Poured	flowed or moved continuously in a steady stream
Pouring	causing (something) to flow in a steady stream from or into a container or place
Pours	to move with a continuous flow
Prepare	to make ready beforehand for some purpose, use, or activity
Prepared	made at an earlier time for later use; made ready in advance
Prepares	to make (someone or something) ready for some activity, purpose, use, etc.
Preparing	making or creating (something) so that it is ready for use
Puddle	a very small pool of usually dirty or muddy water
Pull	to exert force so as to cause an item to move toward the force
Pulled	moved (someone or something) in a direction toward the mover

Pulling	removing (someone or something) from a place or situation
Pulls	removes (something) by gripping it and using force
Push	to press against with force in order to drive or impel
Pushed	used force to move (someone or something) forward or away from oneself
Pushes	forces or tries to force (someone or something) to do something
Pushing	to actively push beyond
Rain	water falling in drops condensed from vapor in the atmosphere
Rained	poured down drops of water
Raining	water falling in drops from clouds in the sky
Rains	large amounts of water that fall in drops
Rainy	showery
Rake	an implement equipped with projecting prongs to gather material (as leaves) or for loosening or smoothing the surface of the ground
Rake	to gather leaves, clear, smooth or prepare with a rake
Raked	gathered leaves, broke apart soil; made ground smooth
Rakes	gathers, loosens, or smoothes with or as if with a rake
Rakes	more than one rake
Raking	gathering leaves, breaking apart soil, making ground smooth
Recycle	to reuse or make (a substance) available for reuse
Recycle bin	a can for trash to be recycled
Recycled	sent (used newspapers, bottles, cans, etc.) to a place where they are made into something new
Recycles	uses (something) again
Recycling	adapting to a new use
Red	a color resembling the color of blood or ripe strawberries
Remove	to change the location, position, station, or residence
Removed	moved or took (something) away from a place
Removes	moves by lifting, pushing aside, or taking away or off
Removing	changing location, station, place
Robin	a small chiefly European thrush resembling a warbler and having a brownish-olive back and orangish face and breast
Robins	more than one robin
Rock	a concreted mass of stony material that comes from the ground
Rocks	more than one rock
Roly-poly bug	a pillbug known by many names—roly poly, wood louse, armadillo bug, potato bug
Roots	underground parts of a seed plant body
Rotten	having rotted: putrid
Rotting	undergoing decomposition from the action of bacteria or fungi
Rough	having a broken, uneven, or bumpy surface

Salty	of, seasoned with, or containing salt; or water from the ocean
Saw	a hand or power tool or a machine used to cut hard material (as wood, metal, or bone) and equipped usually with a toothed blade or disk
Scoop	a deep shovel or similar implement for digging, dipping, or shoveling
Scooped	picked up and moved (something) with a scoop, a spoon, etc.
Scooping	the action of picking up and moving an item with a scoop
Scoops	picks up (something or someone) in one quick, continuous motion
Season	one of the four quarters into which the year is commonly divided
See	to perceive with the eye
Seed	the grain or ripened ovule of a plant used for sowing
Seeds	more than one seed
Sensory garden	a garden to provide combined sensory opportunities for the user such that the user may not normally experience
Shade	shelter (as by foliage) from the heat and glare of sunlight
Shady	giving or providing cover
Shed	to lose (leaves, skin, fur, etc.) naturally
Shed	a building that is used for storing equipment
Sheds	small, simple buildings used especially for storing things
Short	not tall or high; low
Shorter	extending a smaller distance from one end to the other end
Shortest	having the smallest length
Shovel	a hand implement consisting of a broad scoop or a more or less hollowed-out blade with a handle used to lift and throw material
Shovel	to dig or clear with a shovel
Shoveled	dug or cleaned out with a shovel
Shoveling	lifting or throwing material
Shovels	more than one shovel
Shovels	lifts and throws (dirt, sand, snow, etc.) with a shovel
Sky	the upper atmosphere or expanse of space that constitutes an apparent great vault or arch over the earth
Sleet	frozen or partly frozen rain
Sleeting	to send down sleet
Smell	to perceive the odor or scent of through stimuli affecting the olfactory nerves
Smooth	having a continuous even surface
Snow	precipitation in the form of small white ice crystals formed directly from the water vapor of the air at a temperature of less than 32°F (0°C)
Snow drift	banked snow
Snowed	to let fall like snow
Snowing	to descend like snow
Snows	falls as snow crystals

Soft	pleasing or agreeable to the senses
Softer	more pleasing or agreeable to the senses
Softest	most pleasing or agreeable to the senses
Soil	the upper layer of earth that may be dug or plowed in which plants grow
Sound	the sensation perceived by the sense of hearing
Sounds	noises that are heard
Sour	causing or characterized by the one of the four basic taste sensations that is produced chiefly by acids
Spice	any of various aromatic vegetable products (as pepper or nutmeg) used to season or flavor foods
Spices	more than one spice
Spigot	faucet
Spigots	more than one spigot
Spring	a time or season of growth or development; specifically, the season between winter and summer
Springtime	the season of spring
Sprinkle	to scatter in drops or particles
Sprinkling	a light rain
Sprout	a shoot of a plant
Sprouts	more than one shoot of a plant
Squirrel	a small animal having a long bushy tail and strong hind legs
Squirrels	more than one squirrel
Stem	the main trunk of a plant
Stick	a woody piece or part of a tree or shrub
Sticky	coated with a tacky substance
Stream	a body of running water (as a river or brook) flowing on the earth
Streams	more than one stream
Streams	unbroken currents or flow of water
Summer	the season between spring and autumn
Summertime	the summer season or a period like summer
Sun	the luminous celestial body around which the earth and other planets revolve, from which they receive heat and light
Sunlight	the light of the sun: sunshine
Sunny	marked by brilliant sunlight; full of sunshine
Sweet	pleasing to the taste; noted by taste bud receptors at the front of the tongue
Sweeter	more pleasing to the taste
Sweetest	having the highest sugar content, most pleasing to the taste
Tall	high in stature
Taller	higher in stature

Tallest	highest or most formidable in amount, extent, or degree
Taste	to ascertain the flavor of by taking a little into the mouth
Tasty	having a marked and appetizing flavor
Temperature	degree of hotness or coldness measured on a definite scale
Touch	to bring a bodily part into contact with something or someone especially so as to perceive through the tactile sense
Touches	takes into the hands or mouth
Touching	being in contact with (something or someone)
Trail	a marked or established path or route
Trails	more than one trail
Transplant	to lift and reset (a plant) in another soil or situation
Trash	something in a crumbled or broken condition or mass; debris from pruning or processing plant material
Trash bag	a bag that holds materials that have been thrown away
Trash bin	a container that holds materials that have been thrown away
Tree	a woody perennial plant having a single usually elongated main stem generally with few or no branches on its lower part
Trees	more than one tree
Trim	to make neat by cutting or clipping
Trimming	freeing of excess or extraneous matter by cutting
Trims	removes by cutting
Trowel	a scoop-shaped or flat-bladed garden tool for taking up and setting small plants
Trowels	more than one trowel
Twig	a small shoot or branch usually without its leaves
Twigs	more than one twig
Vegetable	usually a herbaceous plant (as the cabbage, bean, or potato) grown for an edible part
Vegetables	more than one vegetable
Warm	having or giving out heat to a moderate or adequate degree
Warmer	having or giving more heat
Warmest	having or giving the most heat
Water	the liquid that descends from the clouds as rain, forms streams, lakes, and seas, and is a major constituent of all living matter and that when pure is odorless, tasteless
Water can	a container that is used to pour water on plants
Watered	sprinkled, moistened, or drenched with water
Watering	pouring water on (something, such as a plant)
Weed	a plant that is not valued where it is growing and is usually of vigorous growth
Weeded	cleared of weeds
Weeding	removing weeds
Weeds	more than one weed

Wheelbarrow	small usually single-wheeled vehicle used for carrying small loads and that is fitted with handles at the rear by which it can be pushed and guided
Wheelbarrows	more than one wheelbarrow
White	of the color of new snow or milk
Wiggle	to move to and fro with quick jerky or shaking motions
Wiggled	proceeded with twisting and turning movements
Wiggles	moves up and down or from side to side with short, quick motions
Wiggling	the act of moving with short, quick motions
Wind	a natural movement of air of any velocity
Windier	having a stronger movement of air
Windiest	having the strongest movement of air
Windy	marked by strong or stronger than usual air currents
Winter	the season between autumn and spring
Wintertime	the season of winter
Worm	any of numerous relatively small, elongated, usually naked and soft-bodied animals (as a grub, pinworm, tapeworm, shipworm, or slowworm)
Worms	more than one worm
Wriggle	to move along by twisting and turning the body, like a worm or snake

Acorn

Bark

Animal

Bird bath

Ant

Bird house

92

Bird houses

Bridge

Branch

Buds

Breeze

Bug

93

Bugs

Camouflage

Bush

Caterpillar

Bushes

Cinnamon sticks

Clay

Dead

Cloudy

Decompose

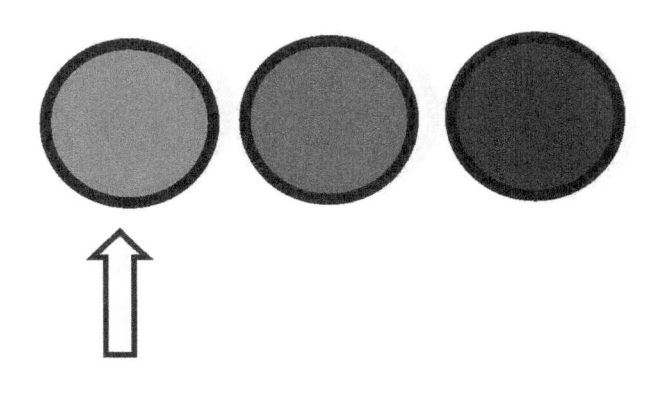

Dark

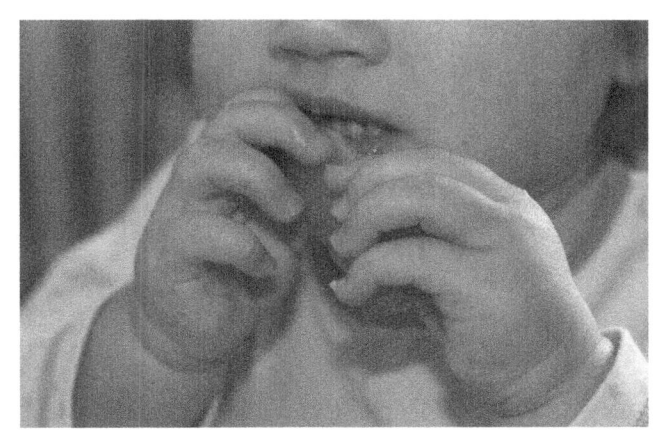

Eat

Environment

Garden

Flower

Goods

Food

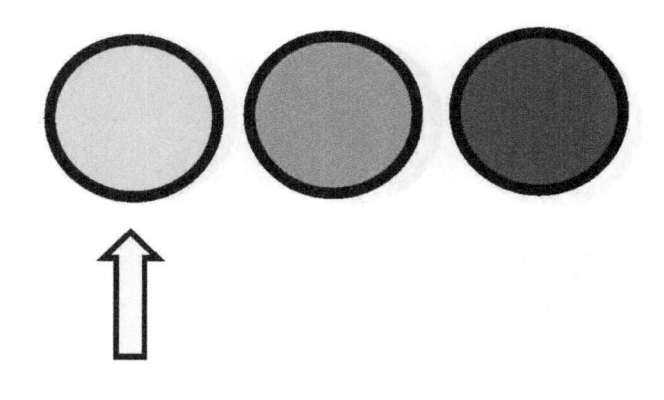

Green

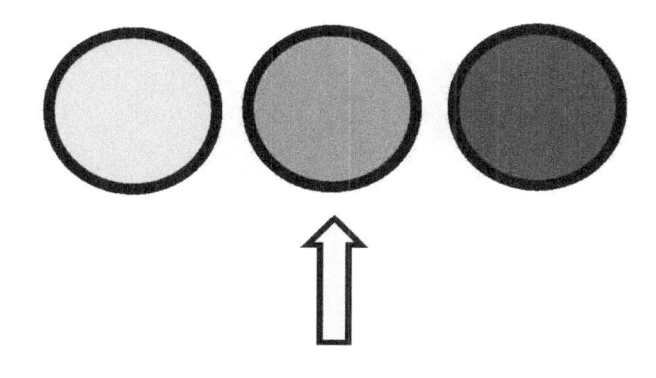

Greener

Habitat

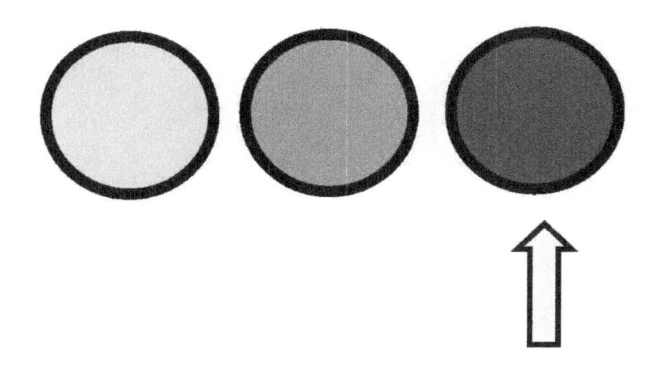

Greenest

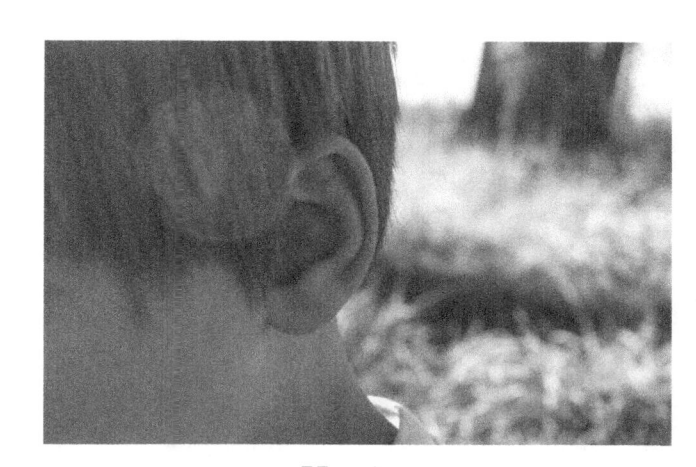

Hearing

Grow

Herbs

Hole

Leaves

Hose

Mix

Lavender

Mud

Mulch

Observe

Mulching

Petal

Nature walk

Pine cone

Pine needle

Planter

Pine tree

Plants

Plant

Potpourri

Pour

Rake

Puddle

Raking

Push

Rock

Rotten

Scoop

Rough

Seed

Salty

Shovel

Smell	Soil
Snowed	Sour
Snowing	Spice

Spices

Sprout

Spigot

Stems

Sprinkling

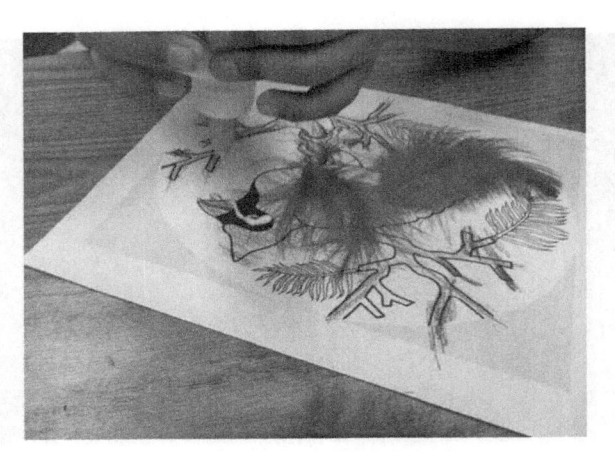

Sticky

104

Summer

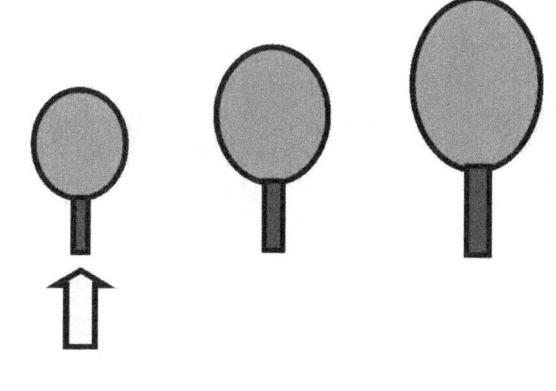

Tall

Sunlight

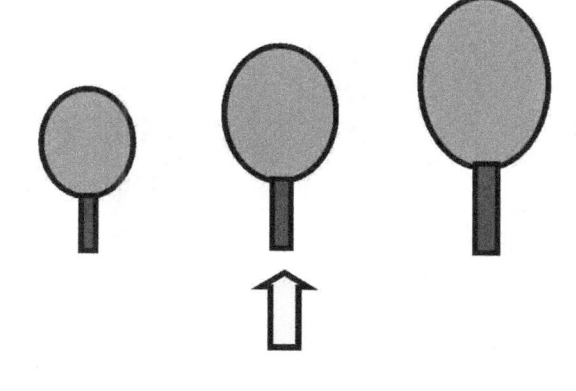

Taller

Sweet

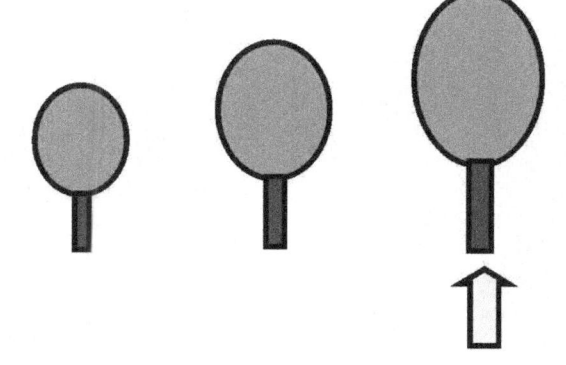

Tallest

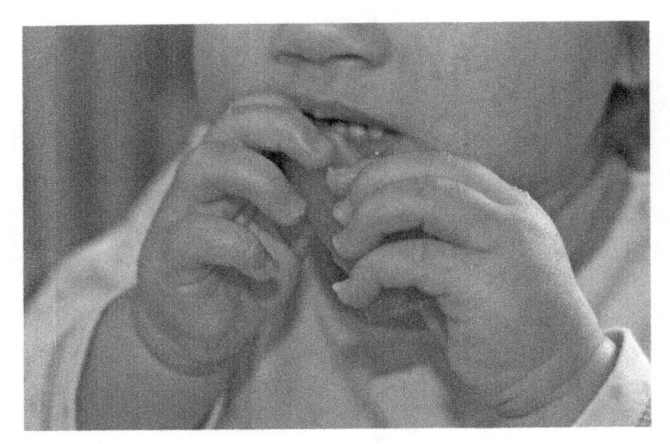

Taste

Trash

Touch

Trash bag

Trail

Tree

Trim

Vegetable

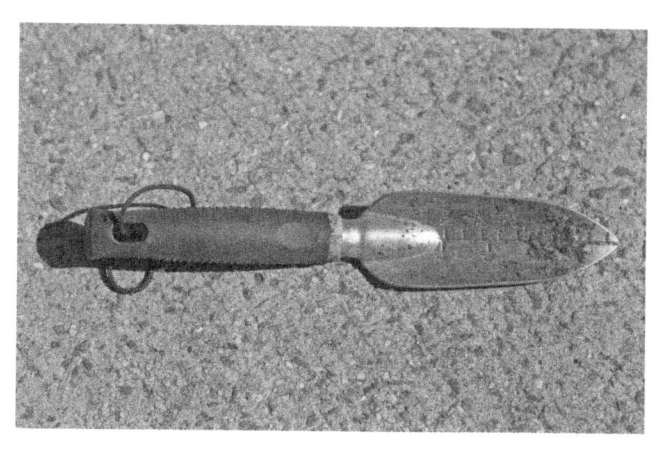

Trowel

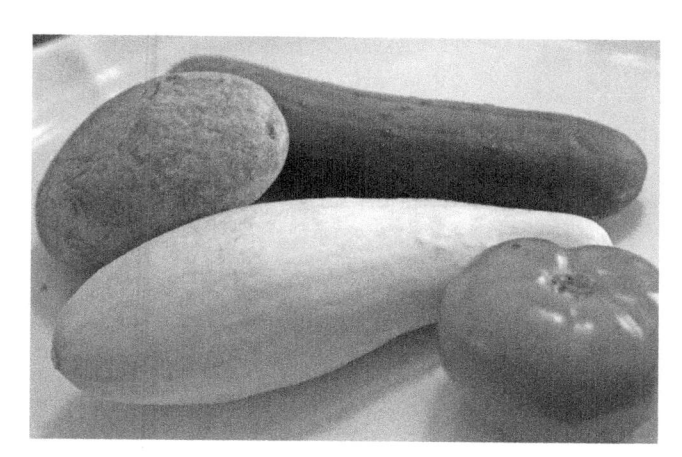

Vegetables

Twig

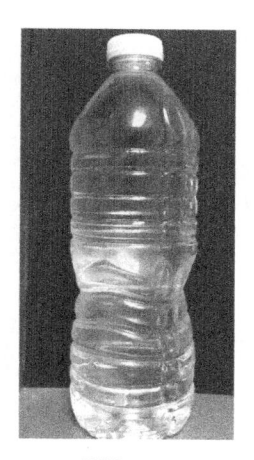

Water

Watering can

Weeding

Weeds

BIBLIOGRAPHY

American Academy of Dermatology. (2013). *Sunscreen FAQs*. Retrieved September 8, 2013, from http://www.aad.org/media-resources/stats-and-facts/prevention-and-care/sunscreens

American Community Gardening Association. (2013). *What Is a Community Garden*. Retrieved September 15, 2013, from http://communitygarden.org/learn/

American Horticultural Therapy Association. (2013). *Horticultural Therapy*. Retrieved September 15, 2013, from http://ahta.org/horticultural-therapy

Better Homes and Gardens. (2012). *How to Care for Garden Tools*. Retrieved September 5, 2013, from http://www.bhg.com/gardening/yard/tools/how-to-care-for-garden-tools/

Bransford, J. D., Brown, A. L., and Cocking, R. R. (eds). (2002). *How People Learn: Brain, Mind, Experience, and School*. Washington, DC: National Academy Press.

Carleton, L. M., and Marzano, R. J. (2010). *Vocabulary Games for the Classroom*. Bloomington, IN: Marzano Research Laboratory.

Centers for Disease Control and Prevention. (2013). *Glossary*. Retrieved September 5, 2013, from http://www2a.cdc.gov/nip/isd/ycts/mod1/scripts/glossary.asp?item=anaphylaxis

Chicago Botanic Garden. (2013). *Horticultural Therapy Services*. Retrieved September 15, 2013, from http://www.chicagobotanic.org/therapy/

Christiansen, C., Baum, C. M., and Bass-Haugen, J. (2005). Person-Environment-Occupation-Performance: An Occupation-Based Framework for Practice. Occupational Therapy: Performance, Participation, and Well-being (242–266). Thorofare, NJ: Slack.

Community Action Coalition for South Central Wisconsin, Inc. (2013). *Madison's Inclusive Community Gardens*. Retrieved September 15, 2013, from http://www.cacscw.org/downloads/CommGardensFinal_UnivDesign.pdf

Dekker, S., Lee, N. C., Howard-Jones, P., and Jolles, J. (2012). Neuromyths in Education: Prevalence and Predictors of Misconceptions among Teachers. *Frontiers in Psychology*, 3(429), 1–8.

Hoogsteen, L., and Woodgate, R. L. (2010). Can I Play? A Concept nalysis of Participation in Children with Disabilities. *Physical and Occupational Therapy in Pediatrics*, 30(4), 325–339.

Husted, K. (2012, February 22). *Can Gardening Help Troubled Minds Heal?* Retrieved September 15, 2013, from http://www.npr.org/blogs/thesalt/2012/02/17/147050691/can-gardening-help-troubled-minds-heal

Laverdure, P. A., and Rose, D. S. (2012). Providing Educationally Relevant Occupational and Physical Therapy Services. *Physical & Occupational Therapy in Pediatrics*, *32*(4), 347–354.

Office of Special Education and Rehabilitative Services, U.S. Department of Education. (2008, May). *Frequently Asked Questions (FAQs) about NIDRR*. Retrieved September 8, 2013, from http://www2.ed.gov/about/offices/list/osers/nidrr/faq.html#question16

U.S. Department of Education, Office of Special Education Programs' (OSEP).(2006, August). Retrieved October 5, 2013, from U.S. Department of Education, Office of Special Education Programs' (OSEP's) IDEA website: http://idea.ed.gov/explore/home.

WETA. All about Adolescent Literacy. (2013). *Frayer Model*. Retrieved September 13, 2013, from http://www.adlit.org/strategies/22369/

ABOUT THE AUTHORS

Tammy R. Blake, OTD, OTR/L, received a Bachelor of Science degree in occupational therapy from Virginia Commonwealth University in Richmond, Virginia. She received her doctorate in occupational therapy from Rocky Mountain University of Health Professions in Provo, Utah. She has worked in the field of occupational therapy since 1992 in a variety of settings including acute and sub-acute rehabilitation centers, residential treatment centers, and public school settings. Over the last decade, she has worked in the public school system and has collaborated with teachers, speech language pathologists, and other occupational therapists for local and regional presentations and workshops.

Dawn M. Leach, M.S. CCC-SLP, received both a Bachelor of Science and a Master of Science degree in speech-language pathology from James Madison University in Harrisonburg, Virginia. She holds a Certification of Clinical Competence in speech-language pathology from the American Speech-Language-Hearing Association; a license from the Commonwealth of Virginia, Department of Health Professions, Board of Audiology and Speech-Language Pathology; and a teaching license from the Commonwealth of Virginia. Since 1990, she has worked in the field of speech-language pathology in the public school setting with students affected by a variety of communication disorders from preschool through high school. She has collaborated with occupational therapists and teachers for presentations at the Virginia Occupational Therapy Association.

Shannon Fenix, M.S., O.T.R./L., received a Bachelor of Science in food, nutrition and exercise from Virginia Polytechnic Institute and State University in Blacksburg, Virginia. She received her Master of Science degree in occupational therapy from Virginia Commonwealth University in Richmond, Virginia. Having worked as an occupational therapist since 2003, she has practiced in acute and sub-acute rehabilitation facilities and private outpatient clinics with both children and adults. For the past ten years, she has worked in the public school system. She has collaborated with teachers and related service providers for program development and shared her experiences with peers in professional presentations.

Lightning Source UK Ltd.
Milton Keynes UK
UKOW06f2341250714

235816UK00014B/333/P

9 781457 526336